U.S.A. TRAVEL GUIDES

NEW JERSEY

BY ANN HEINRICHS • ILLUSTRATED BY MATT KANIA

The Child's World®
childsworld.com

Published by The Child's World®
1980 Lookout Drive • Mankato, MN 56003-1705
800-599-READ • www.childsworld.com

Photo Credits
Photographs ©: ESB Professional/Shutterstock Images, cover, 1; Nicholas A. Tonelli CC2.0, 7; Cambodia4kids.org Beth Kanter CC2.0, 8; North Wind Picture Archives, 11; Carl Anderson/Scandinavian Fest, 12; Jonathan Collins/Shutterstock Images, 15; George Sheldon/Shutterstock Images, 16; Gilbert Stuart/Detroit Publishing Company/Library of Congress, 17; Shutterstock Images, 19, 31, 37 (top), 37 (bottom); Mint Images/Newscom, 20; J. Donaldson/Shutterstock Images, 23; Elizabeth K. Joseph CC2.0, 24; Joseph Sohm/Shutterstock Images, 27; Holly Higgins CC2.0, 28; John Greim/John Greim Photography/Newscom, 32; Bachrach/Library of Congress, 34; Thomas Edison National Historical Park/National Park Service/Department of the Interior, 35

ISBN 9781503819702
LCCN 2016961183

Printing
Printed in the United States of America
PA02334

Ann Heinrichs is the author of more than 100 books for children and young adults. She has also enjoyed successful careers as a children's book editor and an advertising copywriter. Ann grew up in Fort Smith, Arkansas, and lives in Chicago, Illinois.

About the Author
Ann Heinrichs

Matt Kania loves maps and, as a kid, dreamed of making them. In school he studied geography and cartography, and today he makes maps for a living. Matt's favorite thing about drawing maps is learning about the places they represent. Many of the maps he has created can be found in books, magazines, videos, Web sites, and public places.

About the
Map Illustrator
Matt Kania

On the cover: Enjoy amusement park rides and great beach views on the Atlantic City boardwalk.

OUR NEW JERSEY TRIP

NEW JERSEY

All aboard for the Garden State. That's New Jersey! There's so much to see and do there. There's lots to learn, too. Here's a taste of what's to come.

You'll learn about Thomas Edison and Lucy the Elephant. You'll watch George Washington cross the Delaware River. You'll gobble up blueberry pies. You'll make glass with a master glassmaker. And you'll climb a lighthouse named Old Barney.

That's a lot of stuff for one trip. So we'd better hit the road. Just buckle up, and we're on our way!

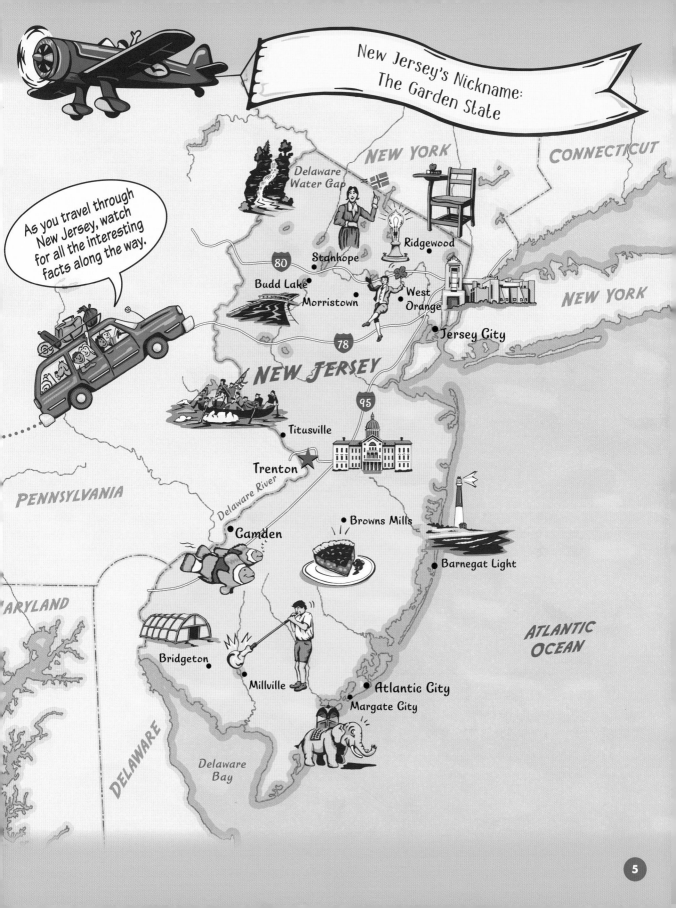

New Jersey's Nickname:
The Garden State

As you travel through New Jersey, watch for all the interesting facts along the way.

NEW YORK

CONNECTICUT

Delaware Water Gap

Ridgewood

Stanhope

Budd Lake

Morristown

West Orange

NEW YORK

Jersey City

NEW JERSEY

Titusville

Trenton

Delaware River

PENNSYLVANIA

Camden

Browns Mills

Barnegat Light

MARYLAND

Bridgeton

Millville

Atlantic City

Margate City

ATLANTIC OCEAN

DELAWARE

Delaware Bay

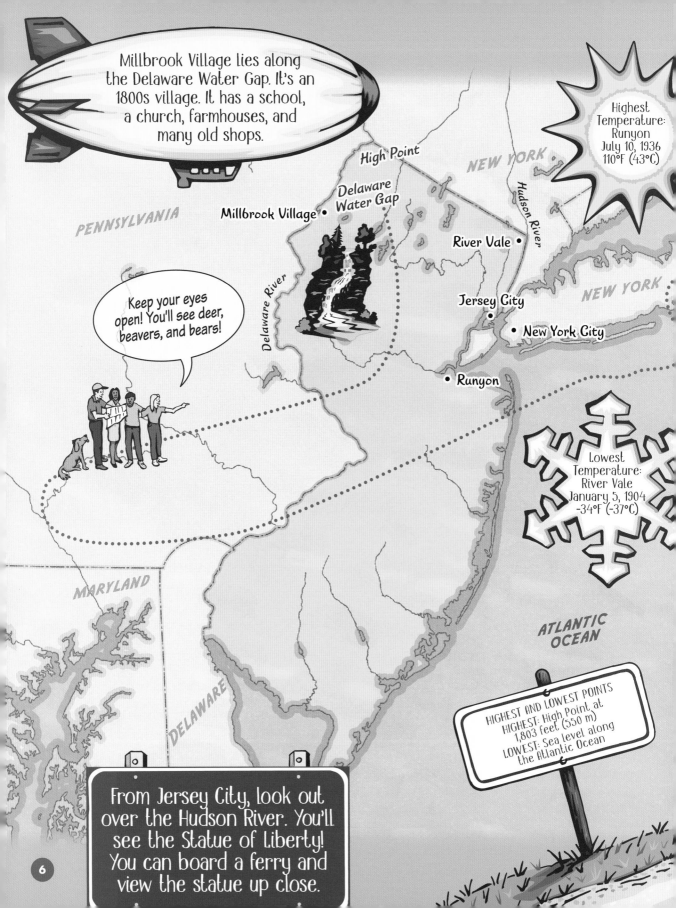

Millbrook Village lies along the Delaware Water Gap. It's an 1800s village. It has a school, a church, farmhouses, and many old shops.

Highest Temperature: Runyon July 10, 1936 110°F (43°C)

High Point

NEW YORK

Delaware Water Gap

Hudson River

Millbrook Village

PENNSYLVANIA

River Vale

NEW YORK

Keep your eyes open! You'll see deer, beavers, and bears!

Jersey City

New York City

Delaware River

Runyon

Lowest Temperature: River Vale January 5, 1904 -34°F (-37°C)

MARYLAND

ATLANTIC OCEAN

DELAWARE

HIGHEST AND LOWEST POINTS
HIGHEST: High Point at 1,803 feet (550 m)
LOWEST: Sea level along the Atlantic Ocean

From Jersey City, look out over the Hudson River. You'll see the Statue of Liberty! You can board a ferry and view the statue up close.

BOATING IN THE DELAWARE WATER GAP

Drift down the river in a boat. Mountains tower above you on both sides. Or hike through the lush forest. You'll come across lakes, ponds, and waterfalls.

This deep valley is the Delaware Water Gap. It's a place to enjoy nature and outdoor fun. The Delaware River flows through this **gorge**. The river carved out the gorge over millions of years.

The Delaware River forms New Jersey's western border. Most of eastern New Jersey faces the Atlantic Ocean. Lots of sandy beaches line the shore. Northeastern New Jersey faces the Hudson River. This area has many busy port cities. New York City lies just across the Hudson.

You'll find lush forests and beautiful scenery along the Delaware Water Gap.

Want to see the world through an elephant's eyes? Just climb up inside Lucy the Elephant. Then look out the windows in her head. They are her eyes!

Lucy the Elephant stands on the beach in Josephine Harron Park in Margate City. She's taller than a six-story building. She weighs as much as ten real elephants.

Once you're inside Lucy, you'll walk up a winding staircase. You'll see that Lucy's all pink inside. The main room has a TV. You can watch videos about Lucy.

Sometimes **hurricanes** smash against Lucy. But she just keeps standing. She's been there for more than 120 years!

Are you at the circus? No, you're just visiting Lucy in Margate City!

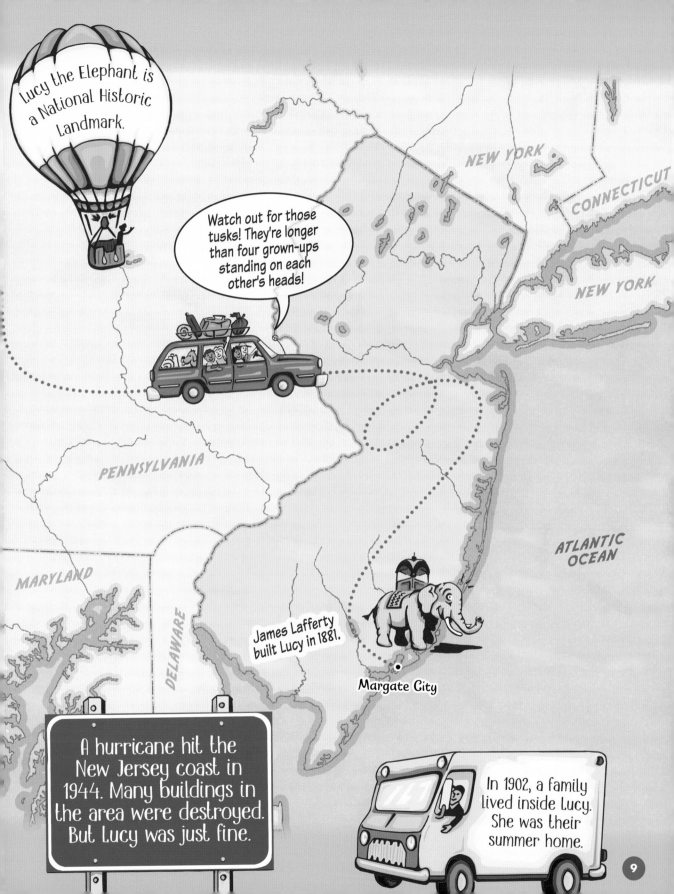

Lucy the Elephant is a National Historic Landmark.

Watch out for those tusks! They're longer than four grown-ups standing on each other's heads!

NEW YORK

CONNECTICUT

NEW YORK

PENNSYLVANIA

ATLANTIC OCEAN

MARYLAND

DELAWARE

James Lafferty built Lucy in 1881.

Margate City

A hurricane hit the New Jersey coast in 1944. Many buildings in the area were destroyed. But Lucy was just fine.

In 1902, a family lived inside Lucy. She was their summer home.

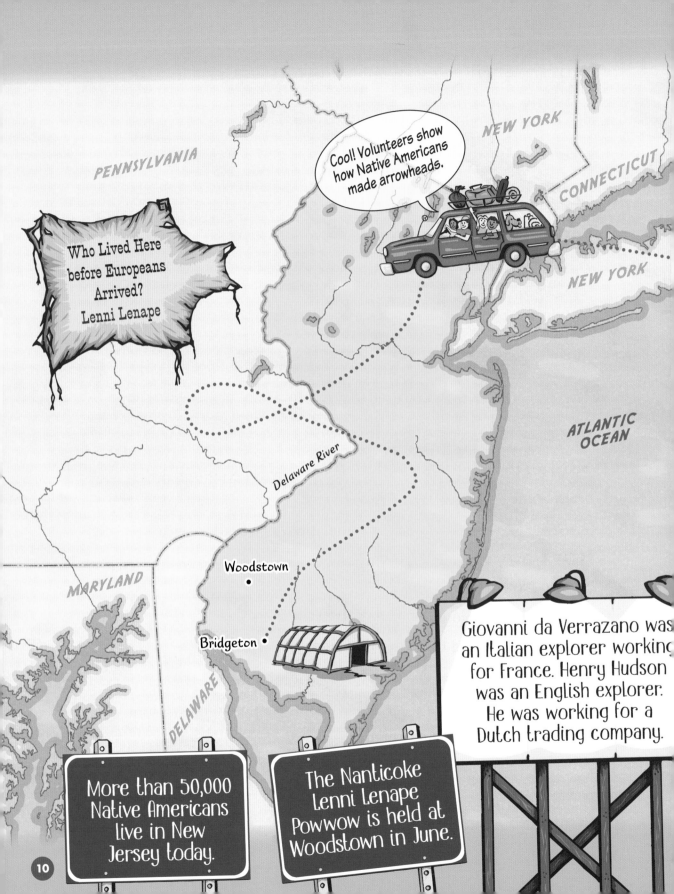

THE WOODRUFF MUSEUM OF INDIAN ARTIFACTS

New Jersey has a rich Native American history. You can learn all about it at the Woodruff Museum of Indian **Artifacts** in Bridgeton. Just walk to the lower level of the Bridgeton Free Public Library. You'll see thousands of Native American arrowheads and other tools. Some of the arrowheads are approximately 10,000 years old!

All of the artifacts in the museum belonged to the Lenni Lenape people. Thousands of Lenape Native Americans once lived in New Jersey. They farmed land along the Delaware River.

European explorers began arriving in the 1500s. Giovanni da Verrazano sailed to the coast in 1524. Henry Hudson arrived in 1609. European settlers bought Lenape lands in the 1700s. They forced the Lenape to move west. Most settled in present-day Oklahoma and Ontario, Canada.

Many Lenni Lenape lived in wooden longhouses along the Delaware River.

SCANDINAVIAN FEST IN BUDD LAKE

Folk dancers twirl on a stage. In a nearby field, you see a large Viking ship. **Blacksmiths** forge traditional Viking weapons. You are at Scandinavian Fest in Budd Lake!

Scandinavia is a region that includes Norway, Denmark, Finland, and Sweden. Many people from New Jersey have Scandinavian roots. Settlers from Sweden and Finland settled in New Jersey in 1638. They formed a **colony** called New Sweden. England took over the region in 1664.

New Jersey's English governors allowed religious freedom. Many English religious groups sailed to New Jersey. There they were free to practice their faith.

Learn more about Scandinavian culture at Budd Lake's Scandinavian Fest.

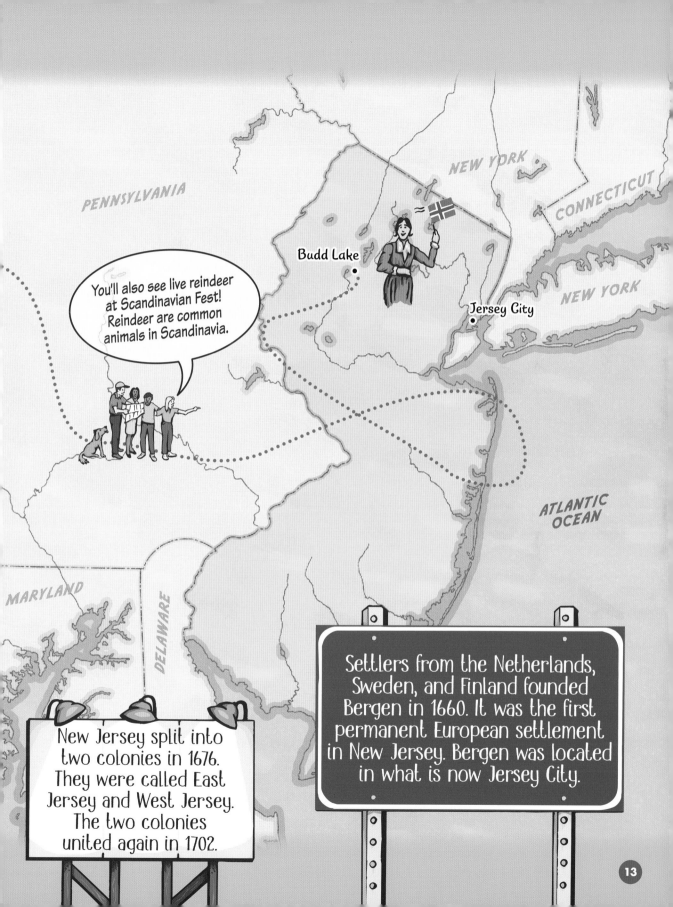

You'll also see live reindeer at Scandinavian Fest! Reindeer are common animals in Scandinavia.

PENNSYLVANIA

NEW YORK

CONNECTICUT

NEW YORK

Budd Lake

Jersey City

ATLANTIC OCEAN

MARYLAND

DELAWARE

New Jersey split into two colonies in 1676. They were called East Jersey and West Jersey. The two colonies united again in 1702.

Settlers from the Netherlands, Sweden, and Finland founded Bergen in 1660. It was the first permanent European settlement in New Jersey. Bergen was located in what is now Jersey City.

Many people who live in New Jersey work in nearby New York City or Philadelphia, Pennsylvania.

Gee... those bagpipes are hard to play. You blow air into the bag and push it out with your arm. Meanwhile, you play a tune.

NEW YORK

CONNECTICUT

• Paterson

Morristown

NEW YORK

• Jersey City

Newark •

• New York City

ATLANTIC OCEAN

PENNSYLVANIA

In 2016, 8,944,469 people lived New Jersey. It's the 11th-large state by population.

• Philadelphia

Newark hosts many events, including the Portugal Day Festival, Puerto Rican Day Parade, African American Heritage Festival, and Brazilian Day Festival.

Saint Patrick is the patron saint of Ireland. Irish people started coming to New Jersey in large numbers in the 1840s.

POPULATION OF LARGEST CITI
Newark.....................281,94
Jersey City.................264,29
Paterson....................147,75

Bagpipes are blaring. Some men are wearing plaid skirts. And everybody's in green. It's the Saint Patrick's Day Parade in Morristown! Saint Patrick's Day is a big Irish holiday.

New Jersey's people belong to many **ethnic** groups. Many came from Italy. Some came from Ireland, Germany, or Russia. Others came from Scotland, Sweden, Poland, or Greece. Many people in New Jersey claim Mexican, Puerto Rican, African, Native American, or Asian roots. Each group has its special music, crafts, and foods.

Saint Patrick's Day parades often feature Scottish Highland bagpipes, the bigger and louder version of the uilleann pipe of Ireland.

WASHINGTON'S CROSSING AT TITUSVILLE

It's Christmastime in Titusville. It's cold and snowy. You stand by the Delaware River, waiting. At last, you see the boat coming. It's George Washington! Well, it's not really George. It's a man dressed like him. He's acting out a famous event in history.

The colonies wanted freedom from Great Britain. So they fought the Revolutionary War (1775–1783). George Washington led the colonies' soldiers. On Christmas, enemy troops camped at Trenton. Washington's camp was across the Delaware River. No one would expect an attack on Christmas. So Washington crossed the Delaware late at night. His surprise attack was a big success! And so was the war.

Watch out—that water looks chilly! Performers reenact Washington crossing the Delaware River.

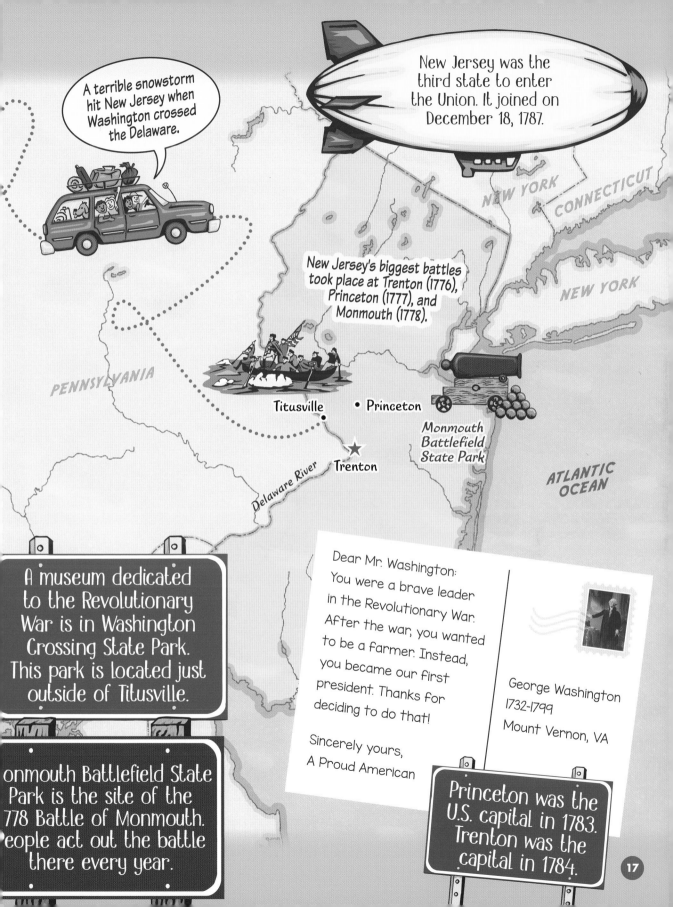

A terrible snowstorm hit New Jersey when Washington crossed the Delaware.

New Jersey was the third state to enter the Union. It joined on December 18, 1787.

NEW YORK

CONNECTICUT

NEW YORK

New Jersey's biggest battles took place at Trenton (1776), Princeton (1777), and Monmouth (1778).

PENNSYLVANIA

Titusville

• Princeton

Monmouth Battlefield State Park

ATLANTIC OCEAN

Delaware River

★ Trenton

A museum dedicated to the Revolutionary War is in Washington Crossing State Park. This park is located just outside of Titusville.

onmouth Battlefield State Park is the site of the 778 Battle of Monmouth. eople act out the battle there every year.

Dear Mr. Washington:
You were a brave leader in the Revolutionary War. After the war, you wanted to be a farmer. Instead, you became our first president. Thanks for deciding to do that!

Sincerely yours,
A Proud American

George Washington
1732-1799
Mount Vernon, VA

Princeton was the U.S. capital in 1783. Trenton was the capital in 1784.

17

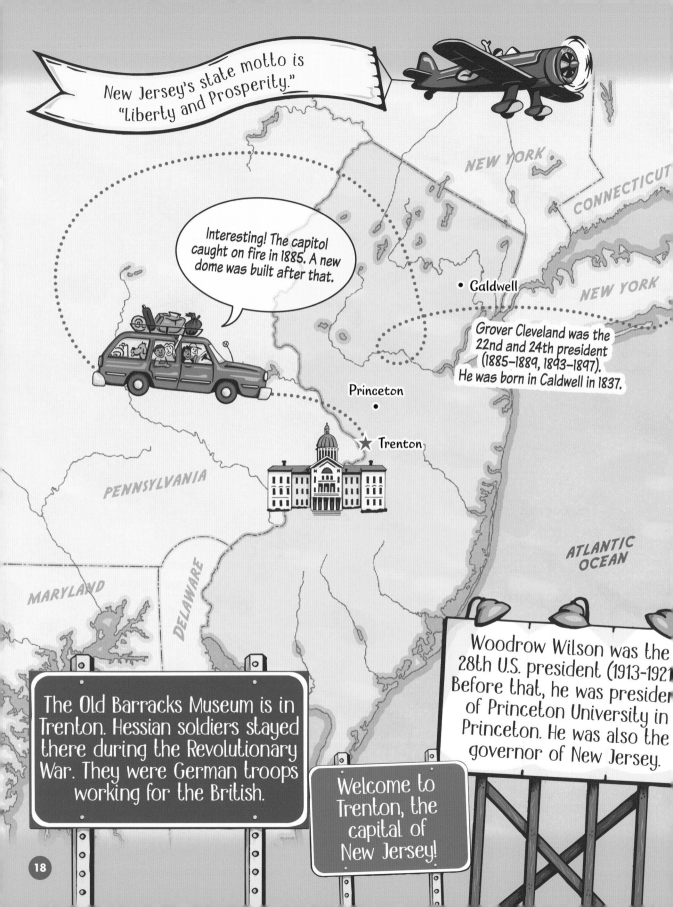

New Jersey's state motto is "Liberty and Prosperity."

Interesting! The capitol caught on fire in 1885. A new dome was built after that.

NEW YORK

CONNECTICUT

NEW YORK

• Caldwell

Grover Cleveland was the 22nd and 24th president (1885–1889, 1893–1897). He was born in Caldwell in 1837.

Princeton
•

★ Trenton

PENNSYLVANIA

ATLANTIC OCEAN

MARYLAND

DELAWARE

The Old Barracks Museum is in Trenton. Hessian soldiers stayed there during the Revolutionary War. They were German troops working for the British.

Welcome to Trenton, the capital of New Jersey!

Woodrow Wilson was the 28th U.S. president (1913–1921) Before that, he was presiden of Princeton University in Princeton. He was also the governor of New Jersey.

THE STATE CAPITOL IN TRENTON

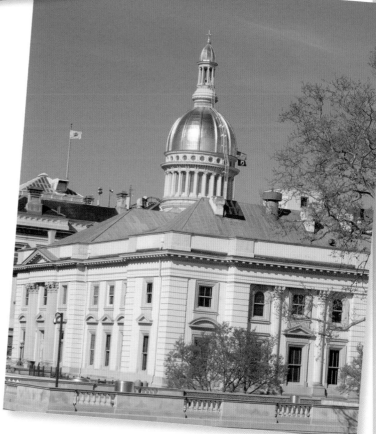

The state capitol has a shiny golden dome. You can see it from far away. It glistens in the sun. It seems to be saying, "This building is important!"

Well, it *is* important. The capitol in Trenton is the center of the state government.

New Jersey's government is divided into three branches. One branch makes the state's laws. It consists of a senate and a general assembly. Another branch makes sure people obey the laws. The governor is the head of this branch. And a third branch is made up of judges. They decide whether laws have been broken.

Look at that gleaming golden dome! You're at the state capitol in Trenton.

Would you like to make a glass **paperweight**? Just visit the Wheaton Arts and Cultural Center in Millville.

You'll see master artists blowing big glass bubbles. You'll watch them bend and shape the glass. It seems like magic! Finally, you'll get to make your own paperweight.

Even in the 1700s, New Jersey had busy factories. These factories were small, and only a few people worked in each. They made cloth and many other products. Today, some big factories are still chugging away. Their products include medicines, foods, and electronics.

It takes a lot of skill to make beautiful glass.

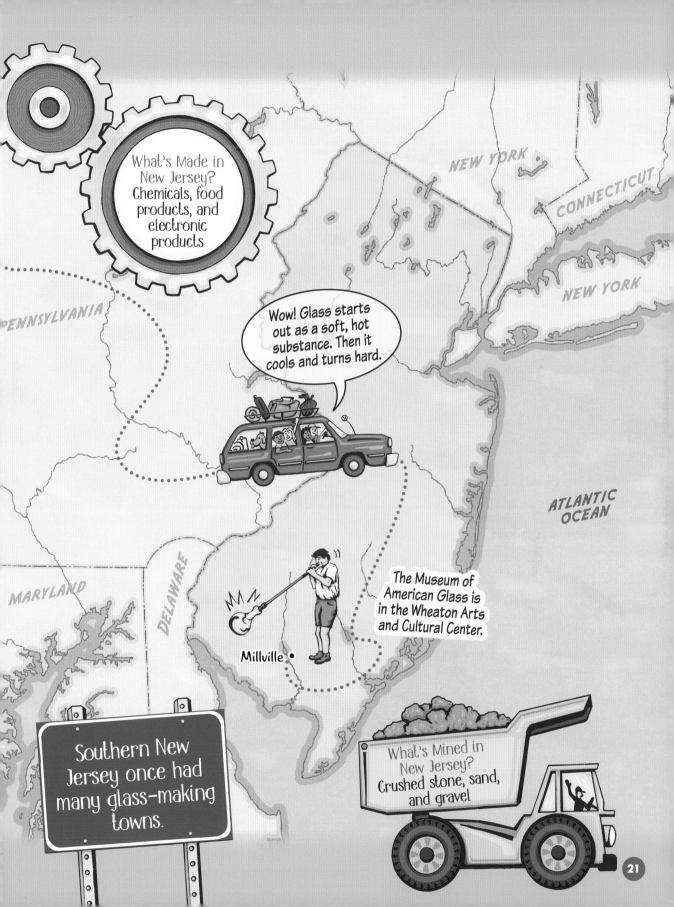

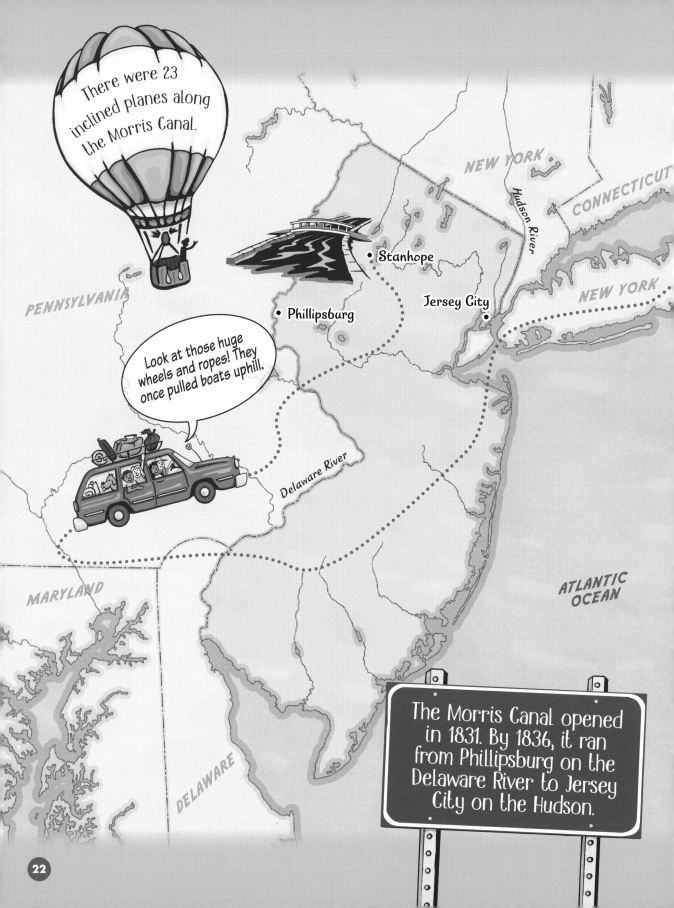

WATERLOO VILLAGE, AN OLD CANAL TOWN

Ever heard of an inclined plane? It's a long, slanted surface. People use them for sliding things up and down. You'll see an inclined plane at Stanhope's Waterloo Village. Boats used to slide on it.

Western New Jersey produced lots of iron. People needed to ship the iron eastward. So they dug the Morris Canal. It joined the Delaware and Hudson rivers. People could ship tons of products on canal boats.

There was only one problem. The canal went over hilly land. Boats could not sail uphill. So they were moved upward on inclined planes.

Waterloo Village was a busy canal town. You'll see its blacksmith shop, school, stores, and homes.

Learn more about canals and New Jersey's shipping history at Waterloo Village.

THE SCHOOLHOUSE MUSEUM IN RIDGEWOOD

What was school like 150 years ago? Visit the Schoolhouse Museum in Ridgewood, and you'll see. There's a potbellied stove for heat. There are reading charts, desks, and maps.

And what's that in the corner? It's a tall stool. That's where naughty kids had to sit. They had to wear a tall, pointy hat. Maybe your school's not so bad after all!

This one-room schoolhouse is a great museum. It displays more than school materials. There are spinning wheels and handmade toys. There's a kitchen from the 1700s. Look around and imagine living back then. Would you have liked it?

You'll receive a lesson in history at Ridgewood's Schoolhouse Museum.

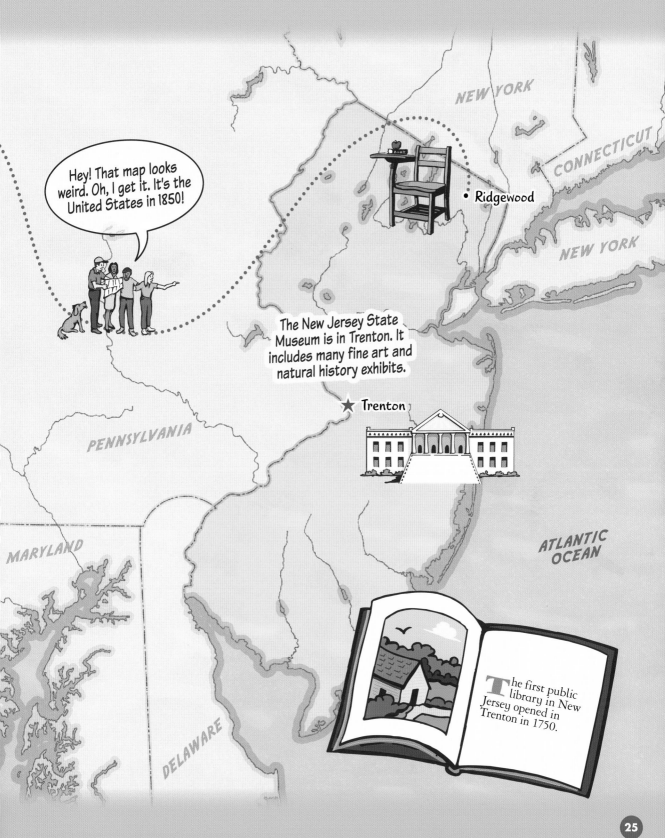

Hey! That map looks weird. Oh, I get it. It's the United States in 1850!

The New Jersey State Museum is in Trenton. It includes many fine art and natural history exhibits.

NEW YORK

CONNECTICUT

NEW YORK

• Ridgewood

★ Trenton

PENNSYLVANIA

MARYLAND

ATLANTIC OCEAN

DELAWARE

The first public library in New Jersey opened in Trenton in 1750.

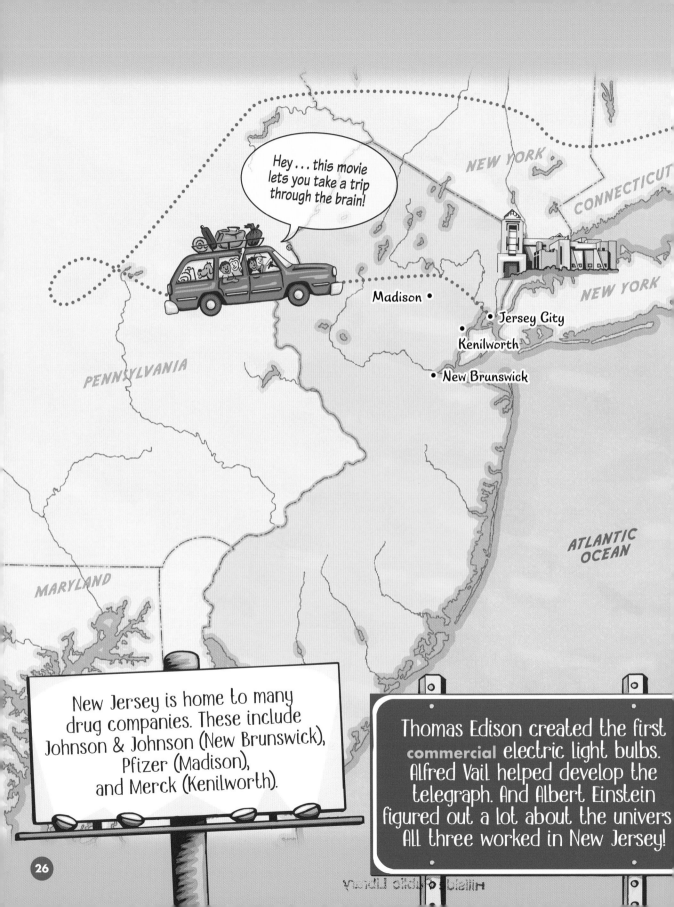

Hey . . . this movie lets you take a trip through the brain!

NEW YORK

CONNECTICUT

NEW YORK

PENNSYLVANIA

Madison •

• Jersey City
•
Kenilworth

• New Brunswick

MARYLAND

ATLANTIC
OCEAN

New Jersey is home to many drug companies. These include Johnson & Johnson (New Brunswick), Pfizer (Madison), and Merck (Kenilworth).

Thomas Edison created the first **commercial** electric light bulbs. Alfred Vail helped develop the telegraph. And Albert Einstein figured out a lot about the univers All three worked in New Jersey!

LIBERTY SCIENCE CENTER IN JERSEY CITY

Want to see a lightning show or talk with a doctor during surgery? Want to see your hair stand straight out? Visit the Liberty Science Center in Jersey City!

Many scientists work in New Jersey. The state's scientists found many uses for chemicals, especially in the 1950s. Scientists use chemicals to make medicines. Other uses include shampoos, soaps, and paint.

Would you like to be a scientist one day? Then Liberty Science Center is a great place to visit. Even science teachers learn a lot there.

Would you make a good scientist? Visit Liberty Science Center and find out.

THE ADVENTURE AQUARIUM IN CAMDEN

Want to touch a stingray? Want to walk above a tank of sharks? How about a sleepover among the fish tanks? Just drop by the Adventure Aquarium in Camden. There's plenty of fun stuff going on there!

This aquarium explores the world's sea life. Some animals there come from New Jersey waters. Others come from far away. One example is a giant Pacific octopus!

Clams, crabs, and lobsters live off of New Jersey's coast. Plenty of fish swim in the rivers and streams. The forests have lots of wildlife, too. There you'll see chipmunks and squirrels. You might see deer, foxes, bears, and rabbits, too. Just watch out for skunks!

Do you like penguins? See penguins perform at Adventure Aquarium's Penguin Island!

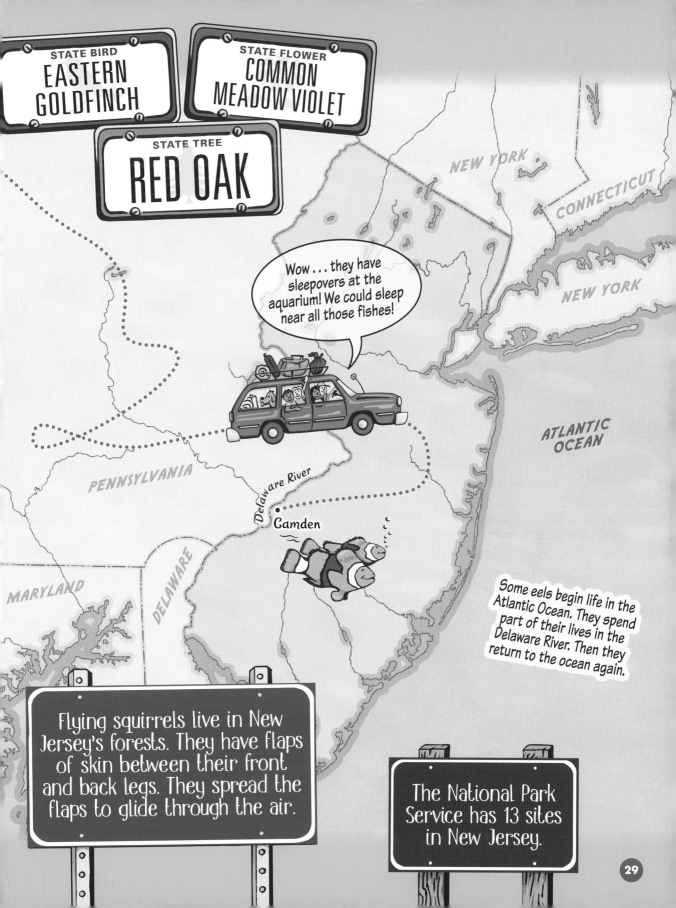

STATE BIRD
EASTERN GOLDFINCH

STATE FLOWER
COMMON MEADOW VIOLET

STATE TREE
RED OAK

NEW YORK

CONNECTICUT

NEW YORK

Wow . . . they have sleepovers at the aquarium! We could sleep near all those fishes!

ATLANTIC OCEAN

PENNSYLVANIA

Delaware River

Camden

MARYLAND

DELAWARE

Some eels begin life in the Atlantic Ocean. They spend part of their lives in the Delaware River. Then they return to the ocean again.

Flying squirrels live in New Jersey's forests. They have flaps of skin between their front and back legs. They spread the flaps to glide through the air.

The National Park Service has 13 sites in New Jersey.

29

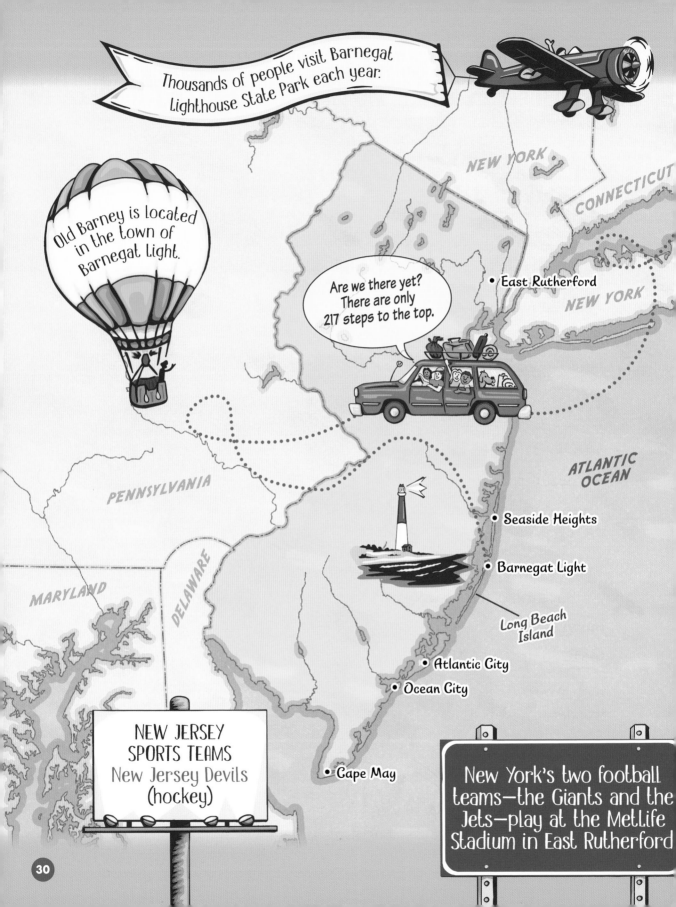

Thousands of people visit Barnegat Lighthouse State Park each year.

Old Barney is located in the town of Barnegat Light.

Are we there yet? There are only 217 steps to the top.

• East Rutherford

NEW YORK

NEW YORK

CONNECTICUT

PENNSYLVANIA

ATLANTIC OCEAN

• Seaside Heights

• Barnegat Light

Long Beach Island

MARYLAND

DELAWARE

• Atlantic City

• Ocean City

NEW JERSEY SPORTS TEAMS
New Jersey Devils (hockey)

• Cape May

New York's two football teams—the Giants and the Jets—play at the MetLife Stadium in East Rutherford

OLD BARNEY ON LONG BEACH ISLAND

Old Barney is a famous site. That's the nickname for Barnegat Lighthouse. It stands on the tip of Long Beach Island. It used to flash signals to passing ships. The signals warned of dangers in nearby waters.

You can climb up inside Old Barney. Look around—you can see for miles. Lots of people visit lighthouses as a hobby.

Strolling along New Jersey's beaches is fun, too. There are many seaside vacation towns. Atlantic City is a famous beach town. So are Cape May, Ocean City, and Seaside Heights. Many beaches have boardwalks. They are just what they sound like—wooden sidewalks!

Planning on taking a boat trip? Old Barney will guide you safely to shore.

THE WHITESBOG BLUEBERRY FESTIVAL IN BROWNS MILLS

How many blueberry pies can you eat? Find out at the Whitesbog Blueberry Festival in Browns Mills. It celebrates New Jersey's state fruit— the blueberry. One fun event is the blueberry pie-eating contest!

New Jersey grows lots of fruits and vegetables. It's a leading state for blueberries and cranberries. But flowers are the state's top crop. In fact, New Jersey is called the Garden State. It grows millions of roses, lilies, and geraniums.

Fishing is another big **industry** in New Jersey. Tons of clams are caught off the coast. So are lobsters, crabs, squid, and fish.

Many farmers harvest blueberries in New Jersey.

Dear Mr. Edison:
You said you wanted to invent "useful things every man, woman, and child in the world wants." And that's just what you did! Thanks for the lights and the movies!

Your pal,
John E. Doe

Thomas Edison
1847-1931
West Orange, NJ

NEW YORK

CONNECTICUT

NEW YORK

• West Orange

Morristown •

PENNSYLVANIA

• Menlo Park

• Princeton

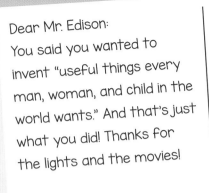

Wow! Thomas Edison was deaf as a young man! He lost all of his hearing when he got older.

Alfred Vail helped develop the telegraph. He was from Morristown.

MARYLAND

ATLANTIC OCEAN

DELAWARE

The Thomas Edison National Historical Park is in West Orange. It preserves Edison's home and lab.

Famous scientist Albert Einstein (1879-1955) worked at the Institute for Advanced Study in Princeton.

Could you be the world's next great inventor? Find out at Thomas Edison National Historical Park! Try building your own electric light bulb. Learn about Thomas Edison and some of his most popular inventions.

Edison was an awesome inventor. He invented 1,093 new things! One was the phonograph record player. Another was motion pictures.

Edison's first **laboratory** was in Menlo Park. He built a bigger lab in 1887. It was in West Orange. Edison called this new lab the Invention Factory. You'll see many of his inventions there. Maybe they'll give you some bright ideas!

Thomas Edison once lived in this house in West Orange.

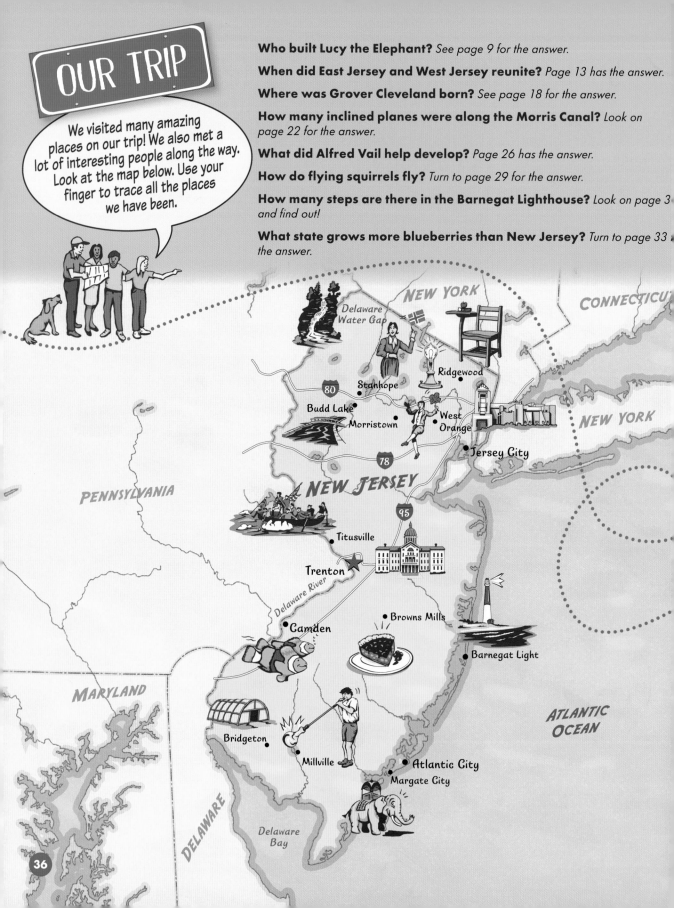

OUR TRIP

We visited many amazing places on our trip! We also met a lot of interesting people along the way. Look at the map below. Use your finger to trace all the places we have been.

Who built Lucy the Elephant? *See page 9 for the answer.*

When did East Jersey and West Jersey reunite? *Page 13 has the answer.*

Where was Grover Cleveland born? *See page 18 for the answer.*

How many inclined planes were along the Morris Canal? *Look on page 22 for the answer.*

What did Alfred Vail help develop? *Page 26 has the answer.*

How do flying squirrels fly? *Turn to page 29 for the answer.*

How many steps are there in the Barnegat Lighthouse? *Look on page 3 and find out!*

What state grows more blueberries than New Jersey? *Turn to page 33 the answer.*

CONNECTICUT

NEW YORK

NEW YORK

Delaware Water Gap

Ridgewood

80

Stanhope

Budd Lake

Morristown

West Orange

78

Jersey City

PENNSYLVANIA

NEW JERSEY

95

Titusville

Trenton

Delaware River

Browns Mills

Camden

Barnegat Light

MARYLAND

Bridgeton

Millville

Atlantic City

Margate City

ATLANTIC OCEAN

DELAWARE

Delaware Bay

STATE SYMBOLS

State animal: Horse

State bird: Eastern goldfinch

State dinosaur: *Hadrosaurus*

State fish: Brook trout

State flower: Common meadow violet

State folk dance: Square dance

State fruit: Blueberry

State insect: Honeybee

State memorial tree: Dogwood

State shell: Knobbed whelk (conch)

State tree: Red oak

State seal

That was a great trip! We have traveled all over New Jersey! There are a few places that we didn't have time for, though. Next time, we plan to visit the Camden Children's Garden. This garden features a greenhouse, a carousel, and a maze. There's even a giant sunflower that's 60 feet (18 m) tall!

STATE SONG

New Jersey has no official state song. The state legislature voted "I'm from New Jersey" as the state song in 1972, but the governor never signed it into law.

"I'M FROM NEW JERSEY"
Words and music by Red Mascara

I know of a state that's a
perfect playland with white
sandy beaches by the sea;
With fun-filled mountains,
lakes and parks, and folks
with hospitality;
With historic towns where
battles were fought, and
presidents have made their
home;
It's called New Jersey, and I
toast and tout it wherever I
may roam.
'Cause . . .

I'm from New Jersey and I'm
proud about it, I love the
Garden State.
I'm from New Jersey and I
want to shout it, I think it's
simply great.

All of the other states
throughout the nation may
mean a lot to some;
But I wouldn't want another,
Jersey is like no other, I'm
glad that's where I'm from.

If you want glamour, try
Atlantic City or Wildwood
by the sea;
Then there is Trenton,
Princeton, and Fort
Monmouth, they all made
history.
Each little town has got that
certain something, from
High Point to Cape May;
And some place like
Mantoloking, Phillipsburg,
or Hoboken will steal your
heart away.

State flag

FAMOUS PEOPLE

Aldrin, Edwin "Buzz," Jr. (1930–), astronaut

Basie, William "Count" (1904–1984), piano player, bandleader

Blume, Judy (1938–), children's author

Burr, Aaron (1756–1836), U.S. vice president under Thomas Jefferson

Cleveland, Grover (1837–1908), 22nd and 24th U.S. president

DeVito, Danny (1944–), actor

Edison, Thomas (1847–1931), inventor

Hathaway, Anne (1982–), actor

Hernandez, Laurie (2000–), gymnast

Houston, Whitney (1963–2012), singer and actor

Jonas, Nick (1992–), singer

Lloyd, John Henry (1884–1965), baseball player

Michele, Lea (1986–), singer and actor

Nicholson, Jack (1937–), actor

O'Neal, Shaquille (1972–), basketball player

Sinatra, Frank (1915–1998), singer

Springsteen, Bruce (1949–), singer, guitarist

Streep, Meryl (1949–), actor

Travolta, John (1954–), actor

Vaughan, Sarah (1924–1990), jazz singer

Whitman, Walt (1819–1892), poet

Willis, Bruce (1955–), actor

Wilson, Woodrow (1856–1924), 28th U.S. president

WORDS TO KNOW

artifacts (ART-uh-fakts) objects that were used by human beings of the past

blacksmiths (BLAK-smiths) people who make metal objects using fire to heat the metal and a hammer to shape it

colony (KOL-uh-nee) a land with ties to a mother country

commercial (kuh-MUR-shuhl) available to the public

ethnic (ETH-nik) relating to a person's race or nationality

gorge (GORJ) land that has been deeply cut by a river

hurricanes (HUR-uh-kaynz) powerful storms that blow in from the sea

industry (IN-duh-stree) a type of business

laboratory (LAB-ruh-tor-ee) a place where scientists work

paperweight (PAY-pur-wate) a heavy object made to hold papers down

TO LEARN MORE

IN THE LIBRARY

Misztal, Maggie. *The Colony of New Jersey.* New York, NY: PowerKids, 2016.

Rogal, Hannah. *New Jersey.* Minneapolis, MN: Bellwether, 2014.

Stanley, Joseph. *Delaware (Lenape).* New York, NY: PowerKids, 2016.

Yasuda, Anita. *Thomas Edison.* New York, NY: AV2 by Weigl, 2013.

ON THE WEB

Visit our Web site for links about New Jersey:

childsworld.com/links

Note to Parents, Teachers, and Librarians: We routinely verify our Web links to make sure they are safe and active sites. So encourage your readers to check them out!

PLACES TO VISIT OR CONTACT

New Jersey Division of Travel & Tourism

visitnj.org
P.O. Box 460
Trenton, NJ 08625
800/847-4865

For more information about traveling in New Jersey

The New Jersey Historical Society

jerseyhistory.org
52 Park Place
Newark, NJ 07102
973/596-8500

For more information about the history of New Jersey

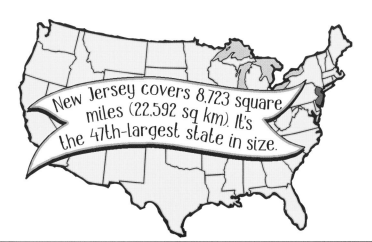

New Jersey covers 8,723 square miles (22,592 sq km). It's the 47th-largest state in size.

INDEX

Bye, Garden State.
We had a great time.
We'll come back soon!